MW00826260

THE
Resilience
JOURNAL

Transcending Turbulent Times Through Journaling

by TERESA BRUNI

Inspiring and uplifting every individual so that they may reclaim their innate right to a healthy, joyful, and abundant life!

Join The 2020 Resilience Journal Project
by visiting www.LessFearMoreFlow.com/Journal

Teresa Bruni

Founder of Less Fear, More Flow LLC and

The 2020 Resilience Journal Project

To contact the author, visit TeresaBruni.com

ISBN: 978-0-9913422-2-8

©2020 Less Fear, More Flow LLC. All Rights Reserved.

No part of this book may be used or reproduced by any means, graphic, electronic, or mechanical, including photocopying, recording, taping or by any information storage retrieval system without the written permission of the author.

> I can shake off everything as I write; my sorrows disappear, my courage is reborn.
>
> — Anne Frank

HOW TO USE YOUR JOURNAL

The decision to begin writing about your life through the process of Journaling, empowers you to actively improve your mental and physical health. Generally available research reveals outcomes showing that written expression of your deepest thoughts and feelings can reduce personal stress. These studies indicate that writing for as little as a few minutes a day is enough to lead to physiological changes such as lowering of blood pressure and reduction of other measurable effects of stress. Journaling has even been shown to decrease your risk of illness by strengthening your immunity, and increasing your ability to heal.

On the first page, rate each topic on a scale of 1-10, with 1 being very poor, and 10 being excellent. In the space provided, write in information you believe is valuable for documenting your day. Your notes may include anything you think is significant, such as global news or personal experiences. It's your choice. This is your Journal.

The second page is for your innermost thoughts and feelings. You may choose to write more, draw or add pictures. You are encouraged to be creative! There are enough pages to document ninety days and extra pages in the back if you need more space.

HEALTH – Rate how you felt physically. Did you feel strong and healthy, or were you tired and achy?

EXERCISE – Did you get some movement that stimulated circulation? Did you go for a walk, do some gardening, practice some yoga, etc.?

NUTRITION – Did you eat healthily and support your body with supplements?

FUN/ENJOYMENT – Did you take time for fun and laughter?

COMMUNITY – Did you enjoy communication with friends and family?

GRATITUDE – Did you find things to be grateful for throughout your day?

SPIRITUALITY – Did you take time to meditate or pray—something to center and support your soul?

CONTRIBUTION – Did you make a positive contribution to the world in some way, such as caring for someone in need?

REST & SLEEP – Good sleep and proper rest are essential. How did you do?

Paper has more patience than people.

— Anne Frank

Date: _____

	1	2	3	4	5	6	7	8	9	10
Health										
Exercise										
Nutrition										
Fun/Enjoyment										
Community										
Gratitude										
Spirituality										
Contribution										
Rest & Sleep										

Notes: _____

_____

_____

_____

_____

_____

_____

_____

Journal Entry

Date: _____

	1	2	3	4	5	6	7	8	9	10
Health										
Exercise										
Nutrition										
Fun/Enjoyment										
Community										
Gratitude										
Spirituality										
Contribution										
Rest & Sleep										

Notes: _____

_____

_____

_____

_____

_____

_____

_____

Journal Entry

Date: _____

	1	2	3	4	5	6	7	8	9	10
Health										
Exercise										
Nutrition										
Fun/Enjoyment										
Community										
Gratitude										
Spirituality										
Contribution										
Rest & Sleep										

Notes: _____

_____

_____

_____

_____

_____

_____

_____

Journal Entry

Date: _____

	1	2	3	4	5	6	7	8	9	10
Health										
Exercise										
Nutrition										
Fun/Enjoyment										
Community										
Gratitude										
Spirituality										
Contribution										
Rest & Sleep										

Notes: _____

_____

_____

_____

_____

_____

_____

_____

Journal Entry

Date: _____

	1	2	3	4	5	6	7	8	9	10
Health										
Exercise										
Nutrition										
Fun/Enjoyment										
Community										
Gratitude										
Spirituality										
Contribution										
Rest & Sleep										

Notes: _____

_____

_____

_____

_____

_____

_____

_____

Journal Entry

Date: _____

	1	2	3	4	5	6	7	8	9	10
Health										
Exercise										
Nutrition										
Fun/Enjoyment										
Community										
Gratitude										
Spirituality										
Contribution										
Rest & Sleep										

Notes: _____

_____

_____

_____

_____

_____

_____

_____

Journal Entry

Date: _____

	1	2	3	4	5	6	7	8	9	10
Health										
Exercise										
Nutrition										
Fun/Enjoyment										
Community										
Gratitude										
Spirituality										
Contribution										
Rest & Sleep										

Notes: _____

_____

_____

_____

_____

_____

_____

_____

Journal Entry

Date: _____

	1	2	3	4	5	6	7	8	9	10
Health										
Exercise										
Nutrition										
Fun/Enjoyment										
Community										
Gratitude										
Spirituality										
Contribution										
Rest & Sleep										

Notes: _____

_____

_____

_____

_____

_____

_____

_____

Journal Entry

Date: _____

	1	2	3	4	5	6	7	8	9	10
Health										
Exercise										
Nutrition										
Fun/Enjoyment										
Community										
Gratitude										
Spirituality										
Contribution										
Rest & Sleep										

Notes: _____

_____

_____

_____

_____

_____

_____

_____

Journal Entry

Date: _____

	1	2	3	4	5	6	7	8	9	10
Health										
Exercise										
Nutrition										
Fun/Enjoyment										
Community										
Gratitude										
Spirituality										
Contribution										
Rest & Sleep										

Notes: _____

_____

_____

_____

_____

_____

_____

Journal Entry

Date: _____

	1	2	3	4	5	6	7	8	9	10
Health										
Exercise										
Nutrition										
Fun/Enjoyment										
Community										
Gratitude										
Spirituality										
Contribution										
Rest & Sleep										

Notes: _____

_____

_____

_____

_____

_____

_____

_____

Journal Entry

Date: _____

	1	2	3	4	5	6	7	8	9	10
Health										
Exercise										
Nutrition										
Fun/Enjoyment										
Community										
Gratitude										
Spirituality										
Contribution										
Rest & Sleep										

Notes: _____

_____

_____

_____

_____

_____

_____

Journal Entry

Date: _____

	1	2	3	4	5	6	7	8	9	10
Health										
Exercise										
Nutrition										
Fun/Enjoyment										
Community										
Gratitude										
Spirituality										
Contribution										
Rest & Sleep										

Notes: _____

_____

_____

_____

_____

_____

_____

Journal Entry

Date: _____

	1	2	3	4	5	6	7	8	9	10
Health										
Exercise										
Nutrition										
Fun/Enjoyment										
Community										
Gratitude										
Spirituality										
Contribution										
Rest & Sleep										

Notes: _____

_____

_____

_____

_____

_____

_____

_____

Journal Entry

Date: _____

	1	2	3	4	5	6	7	8	9	10
Health										
Exercise										
Nutrition										
Fun/Enjoyment										
Community										
Gratitude										
Spirituality										
Contribution										
Rest & Sleep										

Notes: _____

_____

_____

_____

_____

_____

_____

_____

Journal Entry

Date: _____

	1	2	3	4	5	6	7	8	9	10
Health										
Exercise										
Nutrition										
Fun/Enjoyment										
Community										
Gratitude										
Spirituality										
Contribution										
Rest & Sleep										

Notes: _____

_____

_____

_____

_____

_____

_____

_____

Journal Entry

Date: _____

	1	2	3	4	5	6	7	8	9	10
Health										
Exercise										
Nutrition										
Fun/Enjoyment										
Community										
Gratitude										
Spirituality										
Contribution										
Rest & Sleep										

Notes: _____

_____

_____

_____

_____

_____

_____

_____

Journal Entry

Date: _____

	1	2	3	4	5	6	7	8	9	10
Health										
Exercise										
Nutrition										
Fun/Enjoyment										
Community										
Gratitude										
Spirituality										
Contribution										
Rest & Sleep										

Notes: _____

_____

_____

_____

_____

_____

_____

_____

Journal Entry

Date: _____

	1	2	3	4	5	6	7	8	9	10
Health										
Exercise										
Nutrition										
Fun/Enjoyment										
Community										
Gratitude										
Spirituality										
Contribution										
Rest & Sleep										

Notes: _____

_____

_____

_____

_____

_____

_____

_____

Journal Entry

Date: _____

	1	2	3	4	5	6	7	8	9	10
Health										
Exercise										
Nutrition										
Fun/Enjoyment										
Community										
Gratitude										
Spirituality										
Contribution										
Rest & Sleep										

Notes: _____

_____

_____

_____

_____

_____

_____

_____

Journal Entry

Date: _____

	1	2	3	4	5	6	7	8	9	10
Health										
Exercise										
Nutrition										
Fun/Enjoyment										
Community										
Gratitude										
Spirituality										
Contribution										
Rest & Sleep										

Notes: _____

_____

_____

_____

_____

_____

_____

_____

Journal Entry

Date: _____

	1	2	3	4	5	6	7	8	9	10
Health										
Exercise										
Nutrition										
Fun/Enjoyment										
Community										
Gratitude										
Spirituality										
Contribution										
Rest & Sleep										

Notes: _____

_____

_____

_____

_____

_____

_____

_____

Journal Entry

Date: _____

	1	2	3	4	5	6	7	8	9	10
Health										
Exercise										
Nutrition										
Fun/Enjoyment										
Community										
Gratitude										
Spirituality										
Contribution										
Rest & Sleep										

Notes: _____

_____

_____

_____

_____

_____

_____

_____

Journal Entry

Date: _____

	1	2	3	4	5	6	7	8	9	10
Health										
Exercise										
Nutrition										
Fun/Enjoyment										
Community										
Gratitude										
Spirituality										
Contribution										
Rest & Sleep										

Notes: _____

_____

_____

_____

_____

_____

_____

_____

Journal Entry

Date: _____

	1	2	3	4	5	6	7	8	9	10
Health										
Exercise										
Nutrition										
Fun/Enjoyment										
Community										
Gratitude										
Spirituality										
Contribution										
Rest & Sleep										

Notes: _____

_____

_____

_____

_____

_____

_____

_____

Journal Entry

Date: _____

	1	2	3	4	5	6	7	8	9	10
Health										
Exercise										
Nutrition										
Fun/Enjoyment										
Community										
Gratitude										
Spirituality										
Contribution										
Rest & Sleep										

Notes: _____

_____

_____

_____

_____

_____

_____

_____

Journal Entry

Date: _____

	1	2	3	4	5	6	7	8	9	10
Health										
Exercise										
Nutrition										
Fun/Enjoyment										
Community										
Gratitude										
Spirituality										
Contribution										
Rest & Sleep										

Notes: _____

_____

_____

_____

_____

_____

_____

_____

Journal Entry

Date: _____

	1	2	3	4	5	6	7	8	9	10
Health										
Exercise										
Nutrition										
Fun/Enjoyment										
Community										
Gratitude										
Spirituality										
Contribution										
Rest & Sleep										

Notes: _____

_____

_____

_____

_____

_____

_____

Journal Entry

Date: _____

	1	2	3	4	5	6	7	8	9	10
Health										
Exercise										
Nutrition										
Fun/Enjoyment										
Community										
Gratitude										
Spirituality										
Contribution										
Rest & Sleep										

Notes: _____

_____

_____

_____

_____

_____

_____

_____

Journal Entry

Date: _____

	1	2	3	4	5	6	7	8	9	10
Health										
Exercise										
Nutrition										
Fun/Enjoyment										
Community										
Gratitude										
Spirituality										
Contribution										
Rest & Sleep										

Notes: _____

_____

_____

_____

_____

_____

_____

_____

Journal Entry

Date: _____

	1	2	3	4	5	6	7	8	9	10
Health										
Exercise										
Nutrition										
Fun/Enjoyment										
Community										
Gratitude										
Spirituality										
Contribution										
Rest & Sleep										

Notes: _____

_____

_____

_____

_____

_____

_____

_____

Journal Entry

Date: _____

	1	2	3	4	5	6	7	8	9	10
Health										
Exercise										
Nutrition										
Fun/Enjoyment										
Community										
Gratitude										
Spirituality										
Contribution										
Rest & Sleep										

Notes: _____

_____

_____

_____

_____

_____

_____

_____

Journal Entry

Date: _____

	1	2	3	4	5	6	7	8	9	10
Health										
Exercise										
Nutrition										
Fun/Enjoyment										
Community										
Gratitude										
Spirituality										
Contribution										
Rest & Sleep										

Notes: _____

_____

_____

_____

_____

_____

_____

_____

Journal Entry

Date: _____

	1	2	3	4	5	6	7	8	9	10
Health										
Exercise										
Nutrition										
Fun/Enjoyment										
Community										
Gratitude										
Spirituality										
Contribution										
Rest & Sleep										

Notes: _____

_____

_____

_____

_____

_____

_____

Journal Entry

Date: _____

	1	2	3	4	5	6	7	8	9	10
Health										
Exercise										
Nutrition										
Fun/Enjoyment										
Community										
Gratitude										
Spirituality										
Contribution										
Rest & Sleep										

Notes: _____

_____

_____

_____

_____

_____

_____

_____

Journal Entry

Date: _____

	1	2	3	4	5	6	7	8	9	10
Health										
Exercise										
Nutrition										
Fun/Enjoyment										
Community										
Gratitude										
Spirituality										
Contribution										
Rest & Sleep										

Notes: _____

_____

_____

_____

_____

_____

_____

_____

Journal Entry

Date: _____

	1	2	3	4	5	6	7	8	9	10
Health										
Exercise										
Nutrition										
Fun/Enjoyment										
Community										
Gratitude										
Spirituality										
Contribution										
Rest & Sleep										

Notes: _____

_____

_____

_____

_____

_____

_____

_____

Journal Entry

Date: _____

	1	2	3	4	5	6	7	8	9	10
Health										
Exercise										
Nutrition										
Fun/Enjoyment										
Community										
Gratitude										
Spirituality										
Contribution										
Rest & Sleep										

Notes: _____

_____

_____

_____

_____

_____

_____

_____

Journal Entry

Date: _____

	1	2	3	4	5	6	7	8	9	10
Health										
Exercise										
Nutrition										
Fun/Enjoyment										
Community										
Gratitude										
Spirituality										
Contribution										
Rest & Sleep										

Notes: _____

_____

_____

_____

_____

_____

_____

_____

_____

Journal Entry

Date: _____

	1	2	3	4	5	6	7	8	9	10
Health										
Exercise										
Nutrition										
Fun/Enjoyment										
Community										
Gratitude										
Spirituality										
Contribution										
Rest & Sleep										

Notes: _____

_____

_____

_____

_____

_____

_____

_____

Journal Entry

Date: _____

	1	2	3	4	5	6	7	8	9	10
Health										
Exercise										
Nutrition										
Fun/Enjoyment										
Community										
Gratitude										
Spirituality										
Contribution										
Rest & Sleep										

Notes: _____

_____

_____

_____

_____

_____

_____

_____

Journal Entry

Date: _____

	1	2	3	4	5	6	7	8	9	10
Health										
Exercise										
Nutrition										
Fun/Enjoyment										
Community										
Gratitude										
Spirituality										
Contribution										
Rest & Sleep										

Notes: _____

_____

_____

_____

_____

_____

_____

_____

Journal Entry

Date: _____

	1	2	3	4	5	6	7	8	9	10
Health										
Exercise										
Nutrition										
Fun/Enjoyment										
Community										
Gratitude										
Spirituality										
Contribution										
Rest & Sleep										

Notes: _____

_____

_____

_____

_____

_____

_____

_____

Journal Entry

Date: _____

	1	2	3	4	5	6	7	8	9	10
Health										
Exercise										
Nutrition										
Fun/Enjoyment										
Community										
Gratitude										
Spirituality										
Contribution										
Rest & Sleep										

Notes: _____

_____

_____

_____

_____

_____

_____

_____

Journal Entry

Date: _____

	1	2	3	4	5	6	7	8	9	10
Health										
Exercise										
Nutrition										
Fun/Enjoyment										
Community										
Gratitude										
Spirituality										
Contribution										
Rest & Sleep										

Notes: _____

_____

_____

_____

_____

_____

_____

_____

Journal Entry

Date: _____

	1	2	3	4	5	6	7	8	9	10
Health										
Exercise										
Nutrition										
Fun/Enjoyment										
Community										
Gratitude										
Spirituality										
Contribution										
Rest & Sleep										

Notes: _____

_____

_____

_____

_____

_____

_____

_____

Journal Entry

Date: _____

	1	2	3	4	5	6	7	8	9	10
Health										
Exercise										
Nutrition										
Fun/Enjoyment										
Community										
Gratitude										
Spirituality										
Contribution										
Rest & Sleep										

Notes: _____

_____

_____

_____

_____

_____

_____

_____

_____

Journal Entry

Date: _____

	1	2	3	4	5	6	7	8	9	10
Health										
Exercise										
Nutrition										
Fun/Enjoyment										
Community										
Gratitude										
Spirituality										
Contribution										
Rest & Sleep										

Notes: _____

_____

_____

_____

_____

_____

_____

_____

Journal Entry

Date: _____

	1	2	3	4	5	6	7	8	9	10
Health										
Exercise										
Nutrition										
Fun/Enjoyment										
Community										
Gratitude										
Spirituality										
Contribution										
Rest & Sleep										

Notes: _____

_____

_____

_____

_____

_____

_____

_____

Journal Entry

Date: _____

	1	2	3	4	5	6	7	8	9	10
Health										
Exercise										
Nutrition										
Fun/Enjoyment										
Community										
Gratitude										
Spirituality										
Contribution										
Rest & Sleep										

Notes: _____

_____

_____

_____

_____

_____

_____

_____

Journal Entry

Date: _____

	1	2	3	4	5	6	7	8	9	10
Health										
Exercise										
Nutrition										
Fun/Enjoyment										
Community										
Gratitude										
Spirituality										
Contribution										
Rest & Sleep										

Notes: _____

_____

_____

_____

_____

_____

_____

_____

Journal Entry

Date: _____

	1	2	3	4	5	6	7	8	9	10
Health										
Exercise										
Nutrition										
Fun/Enjoyment										
Community										
Gratitude										
Spirituality										
Contribution										
Rest & Sleep										

Notes: _____

_____

_____

_____

_____

_____

_____

_____

Journal Entry

Date: _____

	1	2	3	4	5	6	7	8	9	10
Health										
Exercise										
Nutrition										
Fun/Enjoyment										
Community										
Gratitude										
Spirituality										
Contribution										
Rest & Sleep										

Notes: _____

_____

_____

_____

_____

_____

_____

_____

Journal Entry

Date: _____

	1	2	3	4	5	6	7	8	9	10
Health										
Exercise										
Nutrition										
Fun/Enjoyment										
Community										
Gratitude										
Spirituality										
Contribution										
Rest & Sleep										

Notes: _____

_____

_____

_____

_____

_____

_____

_____

Journal Entry

Date: _____

	1	2	3	4	5	6	7	8	9	10
Health										
Exercise										
Nutrition										
Fun/Enjoyment										
Community										
Gratitude										
Spirituality										
Contribution										
Rest & Sleep										

Notes: _____

_____

_____

_____

_____

_____

_____

_____

Journal Entry

Date: _____

	1	2	3	4	5	6	7	8	9	10
Health										
Exercise										
Nutrition										
Fun/Enjoyment										
Community										
Gratitude										
Spirituality										
Contribution										
Rest & Sleep										

Notes: _____

_____

_____

_____

_____

_____

_____

_____

_____

Journal Entry

Date: _____

	1	2	3	4	5	6	7	8	9	10
Health										
Exercise										
Nutrition										
Fun/Enjoyment										
Community										
Gratitude										
Spirituality										
Contribution										
Rest & Sleep										

Notes: _____

_____

_____

_____

_____

_____

_____

_____

Journal Entry

Date: _____

	1	2	3	4	5	6	7	8	9	10
Health										
Exercise										
Nutrition										
Fun/Enjoyment										
Community										
Gratitude										
Spirituality										
Contribution										
Rest & Sleep										

Notes: _____

_____

_____

_____

_____

_____

_____

_____

Journal Entry

Date: _____

	1	2	3	4	5	6	7	8	9	10
Health										
Exercise										
Nutrition										
Fun/Enjoyment										
Community										
Gratitude										
Spirituality										
Contribution										
Rest & Sleep										

Notes: _____

_____

_____

_____

_____

_____

_____

_____

Journal Entry

Date: _____

	1	2	3	4	5	6	7	8	9	10
Health										
Exercise										
Nutrition										
Fun/Enjoyment										
Community										
Gratitude										
Spirituality										
Contribution										
Rest & Sleep										

Notes: _____

_____

_____

_____

_____

_____

_____

_____

Journal Entry

Date: _____

	1	2	3	4	5	6	7	8	9	10
Health										
Exercise										
Nutrition										
Fun/Enjoyment										
Community										
Gratitude										
Spirituality										
Contribution										
Rest & Sleep										

Notes: _____

_____

_____

_____

_____

_____

_____

_____

Journal Entry

Date: _____

	1	2	3	4	5	6	7	8	9	10
Health										
Exercise										
Nutrition										
Fun/Enjoyment										
Community										
Gratitude										
Spirituality										
Contribution										
Rest & Sleep										

Notes: _____

_____

_____

_____

_____

_____

_____

_____

Journal Entry

Date: _____

	1	2	3	4	5	6	7	8	9	10
Health										
Exercise										
Nutrition										
Fun/Enjoyment										
Community										
Gratitude										
Spirituality										
Contribution										
Rest & Sleep										

Notes: _____

_____

_____

_____

_____

_____

_____

_____

Journal Entry

Date: _____

	1	2	3	4	5	6	7	8	9	10
Health										
Exercise										
Nutrition										
Fun/Enjoyment										
Community										
Gratitude										
Spirituality										
Contribution										
Rest & Sleep										

Notes: _____

_____

_____

_____

_____

_____

_____

_____

Journal Entry

Date: _____

	1	2	3	4	5	6	7	8	9	10
Health										
Exercise										
Nutrition										
Fun/Enjoyment										
Community										
Gratitude										
Spirituality										
Contribution										
Rest & Sleep										

Notes: _____

_____

_____

_____

_____

_____

_____

_____

Journal Entry

Date: _____

	1	2	3	4	5	6	7	8	9	10
Health										
Exercise										
Nutrition										
Fun/Enjoyment										
Community										
Gratitude										
Spirituality										
Contribution										
Rest & Sleep										

Notes: _____

_____

_____

_____

_____

_____

_____

_____

Journal Entry

Date: _____

	1	2	3	4	5	6	7	8	9	10
Health										
Exercise										
Nutrition										
Fun/Enjoyment										
Community										
Gratitude										
Spirituality										
Contribution										
Rest & Sleep										

Notes: _____

_____

_____

_____

_____

_____

_____

_____

Journal Entry

Date: _____

	1	2	3	4	5	6	7	8	9	10
Health										
Exercise										
Nutrition										
Fun/Enjoyment										
Community										
Gratitude										
Spirituality										
Contribution										
Rest & Sleep										

Notes: _____

_____

_____

_____

_____

_____

_____

_____

Journal Entry

Date: _____

	1	2	3	4	5	6	7	8	9	10
Health										
Exercise										
Nutrition										
Fun/Enjoyment										
Community										
Gratitude										
Spirituality										
Contribution										
Rest & Sleep										

Notes: _____

_____

_____

_____

_____

_____

_____

_____

Journal Entry

Date: _____

	1	2	3	4	5	6	7	8	9	10
Health										
Exercise										
Nutrition										
Fun/Enjoyment										
Community										
Gratitude										
Spirituality										
Contribution										
Rest & Sleep										

Notes: _____

_____

_____

_____

_____

_____

_____

_____

Journal Entry

Date: _____

	1	2	3	4	5	6	7	8	9	10
Health										
Exercise										
Nutrition										
Fun/Enjoyment										
Community										
Gratitude										
Spirituality										
Contribution										
Rest & Sleep										

Notes: _____

_____

_____

_____

_____

_____

_____

_____

Journal Entry

Date: _____

	1	2	3	4	5	6	7	8	9	10
Health										
Exercise										
Nutrition										
Fun/Enjoyment										
Community										
Gratitude										
Spirituality										
Contribution										
Rest & Sleep										

Notes: _____

_____

_____

_____

_____

_____

_____

_____

Journal Entry

Date: _____

	1	2	3	4	5	6	7	8	9	10
Health										
Exercise										
Nutrition										
Fun/Enjoyment										
Community										
Gratitude										
Spirituality										
Contribution										
Rest & Sleep										

Notes: _____

_____

_____

_____

_____

_____

_____

_____

Journal Entry

Date: _____

	1	2	3	4	5	6	7	8	9	10
Health										
Exercise										
Nutrition										
Fun/Enjoyment										
Community										
Gratitude										
Spirituality										
Contribution										
Rest & Sleep										

Notes: _____

_____

_____

_____

_____

_____

_____

_____

Journal Entry

Date: _____

	1	2	3	4	5	6	7	8	9	10
Health										
Exercise										
Nutrition										
Fun/Enjoyment										
Community										
Gratitude										
Spirituality										
Contribution										
Rest & Sleep										

Notes: _____

_____

_____

_____

_____

_____

_____

_____

Journal Entry

Date: _____

	1	2	3	4	5	6	7	8	9	10
Health										
Exercise										
Nutrition										
Fun/Enjoyment										
Community										
Gratitude										
Spirituality										
Contribution										
Rest & Sleep										

Notes: _____

_____

_____

_____

_____

_____

_____

_____

Journal Entry

Date: _____

	1	2	3	4	5	6	7	8	9	10
Health										
Exercise										
Nutrition										
Fun/Enjoyment										
Community										
Gratitude										
Spirituality										
Contribution										
Rest & Sleep										

Notes: _____

_____

_____

_____

_____

_____

_____

_____

Journal Entry

Date: _____

	1	2	3	4	5	6	7	8	9	10
Health										
Exercise										
Nutrition										
Fun/Enjoyment										
Community										
Gratitude										
Spirituality										
Contribution										
Rest & Sleep										

Notes: _____

_____

_____

_____

_____

_____

_____

_____

Journal Entry

Date: _____

	1	2	3	4	5	6	7	8	9	10
Health										
Exercise										
Nutrition										
Fun/Enjoyment										
Community										
Gratitude										
Spirituality										
Contribution										
Rest & Sleep										

Notes: _____

_____

_____

_____

_____

_____

_____

_____

Journal Entry

Date: _____

	1	2	3	4	5	6	7	8	9	10
Health										
Exercise										
Nutrition										
Fun/Enjoyment										
Community										
Gratitude										
Spirituality										
Contribution										
Rest & Sleep										

Notes: _____

_____

_____

_____

_____

_____

_____

_____

_____

Journal Entry

Date: _____

	1	2	3	4	5	6	7	8	9	10
Health										
Exercise										
Nutrition										
Fun/Enjoyment										
Community										
Gratitude										
Spirituality										
Contribution										
Rest & Sleep										

Notes: _____

_____

_____

_____

_____

_____

_____

_____

_____

Journal Entry

Date: _____

	1	2	3	4	5	6	7	8	9	10
Health										
Exercise										
Nutrition										
Fun/Enjoyment										
Community										
Gratitude										
Spirituality										
Contribution										
Rest & Sleep										

Notes: _____

_____

_____

_____

_____

_____

_____

Journal Entry

Date: _____

	1	2	3	4	5	6	7	8	9	10
Health										
Exercise										
Nutrition										
Fun/Enjoyment										
Community										
Gratitude										
Spirituality										
Contribution										
Rest & Sleep										

Notes: _____

_____

_____

_____

_____

_____

_____

_____

Journal Entry

Date: _____

	1	2	3	4	5	6	7	8	9	10
Health										
Exercise										
Nutrition										
Fun/Enjoyment										
Community										
Gratitude										
Spirituality										
Contribution										
Rest & Sleep										

Notes: _____

_____

_____

_____

_____

_____

_____

_____

Journal Entry

Date: _____

	1	2	3	4	5	6	7	8	9	10
Health										
Exercise										
Nutrition										
Fun/Enjoyment										
Community										
Gratitude										
Spirituality										
Contribution										
Rest & Sleep										

Notes: _____

_____

_____

_____

_____

_____

_____

_____

Journal Entry

Date: _____

	1	2	3	4	5	6	7	8	9	10
Health										
Exercise										
Nutrition										
Fun/Enjoyment										
Community										
Gratitude										
Spirituality										
Contribution										
Rest & Sleep										

Notes: _____

_____

_____

_____

_____

_____

_____

_____

Journal Entry

Date: _____

	1	2	3	4	5	6	7	8	9	10
Health										
Exercise										
Nutrition										
Fun/Enjoyment										
Community										
Gratitude										
Spirituality										
Contribution										
Rest & Sleep										

Notes: _____

_____

_____

_____

_____

_____

_____

_____

Journal Entry

Date: _____

	1	2	3	4	5	6	7	8	9	10
Health										
Exercise										
Nutrition										
Fun/Enjoyment										
Community										
Gratitude										
Spirituality										
Contribution										
Rest & Sleep										

Notes: _____

_____

_____

_____

_____

_____

_____

_____

Journal Entry

Date: _____

	1	2	3	4	5	6	7	8	9	10
Health										
Exercise										
Nutrition										
Fun/Enjoyment										
Community										
Gratitude										
Spirituality										
Contribution										
Rest & Sleep										

Notes: _____

_____

_____

_____

_____

_____

_____

_____

Journal Entry

Date: _____

	1	2	3	4	5	6	7	8	9	10
Health										
Exercise										
Nutrition										
Fun/Enjoyment										
Community										
Gratitude										
Spirituality										
Contribution										
Rest & Sleep										

Notes: _____

_____

_____

_____

_____

_____

_____

_____

Journal Entry

SECTION II

Date: _____

Date: _____

Date: _____

Date: _____

Date: _____

Date: _____

Date: _____

Date: _____

Date: _____

Date: _____

Date: _____

Date: _____

Date: _____

Date: _____

Date: _____

Date: _____

Date: _____

Date: _____

Date: _____

Date: _____

Date: _____

Date: _____

Date: _____

Date: _____

Date: _____

Date: _____

Date: _____

Date: _____

Date: _____

Date: _____

Date: _____

Date: _____

Date: _____

Date: _____

CPSIA information can be obtained
at www.ICGtesting.com
Printed in the USA
BVHW041421250520
580200BV00012B/194